green books.

Emily Stew
With Some Side Dishes

BY
Thomas Rockwell

ILLUSTRATED BY
David McPhail

 ROARING BROOK PRESS·NEW YORK

For Emily.
—TR

Text copyright © 2010 by Thomas Rockwell

Illustrations copyright © 2010 by David McPhail

Published by Roaring Brook Press

Roaring Brook Press is a division of Holtzbrinck Publishing Holdings Limited

Partnership

175 Fifth Avenue, New York, New York 10010

www.roaringbrookpress.com

Distributed in Canada by H. B. Fenn and Company Ltd.

Cataloging-in-Publication Data is on file at the Library of Congress

ISBN: 978-1-59643-336-6

Roaring Brook Press books are available for special promotions and premiums.
For details contact: Director of Special Markets, Holtzbrinck Publishers.

First Edition March 2010

Book design by Scott Myles

Printed in February 2010 in the United States of America by Worzalla,
Stevens Point, Wisconsin.

2 4 6 8 10 9 7 5 3 1

Table of Contents

A Salmon Sky

Emily Song
sang all day long,
but like a stone,
she made no sound.
Emily Song
sang in her mind,
fabulous songs,
of roses so big
she could sleep in their arms
and climb on their thorns,
of fishes that walked
on four legs on the land,
some even wore shoes
and danced on the sand.
But Emily dear,
her mother would say,
I'd like to hear too.
Oh Ma, she would cry,
the best songs are still.
All the dragons come out
and sit on the hills,
and nobody cares
if you sing while you eat
and laugh in your milk
and keep time with your feet.

Toad Math

Emily Pemily
ate a fat toad.

When she saw what she had done,
she ate another twenty-one.

Then Emily was full of toads.
Toads hung out of her ears and nose.

Who believes Emily ate forty toads?
No one,
except one of the toads.

He is missing a wart
and sits in the dark,
croaking, Emily ate my wart.

I *didn't*! she yells.
You can't count.

1, 2, 5, 8, 3,
croaked the toad.
Don't touch me,
or you'll get them too.

Toad stew, toad stew,
sang Emily, dancing about
in her father's shoes,

till the toad hid under a bramble bush
and croaked to himself
till he fell asleep,
1, 2, 9, 8, 3, 52.

A Nursery Romance

Emily Beanbag
fell in love with Frederick Floursack.
She gazed at him from the nursery windowsill
and he at her from the clothesline,
where he undulated emptily:
Van de Water's Best.
And then she wept. What destiny awaited him?
A mechanic's nose rag?
To stuff a shed window in November's sleet?
Her own father, having lost his beans,
had ended as a polisher of doorknobs.
Emily shrank into herself as the Mistress
took the clothespins off Frederick
and dropped him into the laundry basket.
Now all Emily could see was his crumpled V.

Four days and four nights passed.
Emily was used to being thrown about
and even liked sliding down walls
if she hadn't been thrown so hard
her stitches ached,
but she wasn't used to feeling things as heavily
as if someone had filled her with BB shot.
But on the morning of the fifth day
a package came, and in it
was a handsome pillow with a thick red fringe

all around it and in the center his—
oh his! bright blue star
and on the back *Van de Water's Best*!
and nestled in the tissue paper all around him!
five little beanbags! And so Frederick
and Emily and their five little beanbags
lived happily ever after, all huddled together
in a corner of the big brown chair by the window—
except for the Dismally Hairy Time,
when a new dog used to sneak in and sleep on them
during the long hot summer afternoons.

The Thief

Emily Cutpurse was not a thief herself,
but she had a cat who stole fish.
On Sunday it stole a cod from Emily's sister's mother-in-law
while she was saying grace
(she always said grace with her eyes shut).
In the previous week it had stolen a trout
and a salmon and a dace.
When Emily's father said, Well, we'll eat steak—
the cat stole that too,
and four lamb chops and even three veal cutlets
Emily's mother had just breaded
for the ASPCA potluck supper.
Vegetables! cried Emily's father.
No cat—(and here he eyed the cat,
which was sitting on the sideboard washing its whiskers)—
no cat eats vegetables.
But before anyone could congratulate Emily's father
on his perspicacity, the cat had stolen a potato,
dashing through the creamed turnips to do so.
I don't want to say there was rage and turmoil and bad manners
at the table, because Emily's family were considered
"nice people," but there was certainly a commotion
during which the table was overturned.
So then the cat was forbidden to eat with the family.
But if anyone opened the door to the kitchen, even a crack,
for instance so Mother could pass in the salad course,

the cat dashed through and stole whatever it could,
even Emily's grandmother's wig.
So a family council was held,
during which the cat snuck in and stole the gavel
and then Emily's grandmother's chewing gum,
which she had stuck on the arm of her chair
while she adjusted her false teeth.
So the police were called,
but the cat ate all their sandwiches out of the patrol car
while they were inside writing out the complaint,
and when they went back inside to call for reinforcements,
it stole the patrol car and raced away,
never to be see again.
And so Emily bought a cat who ate only eggs
and was only a nuisance at breakfast
(unless Emily's mother was serving oatmeal)
and when Emily's grandmother gave herself an egg facial.

What Does a Nose Flattened Against a Window Mean?

Emily Tears was so sad and bored
that when it rained,
she thought the summer was weeping
because in four months it would be winter
and everything frozen and glum,
the wind sweeping the ice on the pond bare,
the cows' nostrils steaming,
and Christmas still too far away
to even *try* to wait for.
So Emily would feel teary
and flatten her nose against the window
and wonder about nothing,
because if someone held out both fists to you
and said which fist has the candy,
then in the other fist there was nothing,
so it was something. Moper,
said her mother. Would you please
go into the living room and do nothing?
But don't watch television.
That's worse than nothing.

Malarkey

Alfred Emily
(or Emily in Bill Malarkey's clothes)
was a tough guy—
with two fists painted red (for blood)
and a wart on her nose.
I want to fight, she said
and went out in the backyard
and shadowboxed with the iris
because they were almost her size
and had beards.
She gave up table manners
and swaggered in the hall mirror
(but nobody was home but her mother,
who was upstairs with a headache).
Then she went out on the street
and was discouraged,
because Mrs. Malarkey came along
and said, Emily Jane,
why are you wearing Billy's T-shirt?
I'm sure I left it on the line.
So she grabbed Alfred Emily by the belt
and took back the T-shirt.
So there was Alfred Emily in the middle of the street
with nothing on above her waist
but her tightly crossed arms.

Teef

Little Ned had no front teeth.
I don't mind, but the others teeth.
You mean tease, said his mother.
Now *you're* doing it! yelled Ned.
But if I don't understand?
You pretend, said Ned.

Hogback

Emily Tatner didn't ride a horse, she rode a hog.

It frustrated her so. Sometimes she and her dog—

she always rode with her dog because she was afraid of the hog—

didn't ride anywhere for two days except to the trough.

Why can't I have a *horse*? she would scream at her father.

Because I don't raise horses, I raise hogs.

Sarah Nesheiwat's father raises chickens,

but she doesn't have to ride a *hen*!

Emily began to cry. People laugh at me.

They call out, Be sure to slide off before the slaughterhouse.

But then Hog got up and shook off his mud.

I'll lose my job as Emily's horse.

How long then before I'm a chop?

So he took Emily trit-trot, trit-trot

under the horses' bellies right to the front row

of the fake fox hunt. And then they were off!

Tally-ho! Tally-ho! Hog couldn't leap as well as a horse
but he could go under a gate with a lot less fuss
and smell out holes and burrow through bushes
and sniff the breeze and shoulder dogs,
and finally bite the bag which was the fox
and hold it up in his panting snout.

Tally-ho, hurrah, it's Emily's hog who gets the prize!
But where's Emily? She's three miles back,
tramping home in the roiling dust.
I'll never ride that hog again! I *won't*! *I won't!*

The Richest Girl in the World

Princess Emily Elizabeth Margaret Onion
Augustus Montague von Esterhazy
was lazy.
She would take off her hat made of one-hundred dollar bills
and say, Why should I learn math,
when I can hire forty mathematicians?
Why should I learn to read,
when I can hire the best readers
in Yiddish, French, Latin, what-have-you?
And then she would look down at her platter
of quail stuffed with raspberries flown in
from an Austrian king's garden
and say, Why should I eat,
when I can hire eaters in the drought-stricken regions
who'll pay *me*?
So she wasted away from boredom
and was only reclaimed when a tiger ate *her*,
exclaiming as she vanished,
This is a new sensation,
and it cost nothing.

A Splendor of Diamonds
and Dollars

Emily played the piano
and sang soprano
till the neighbors moved to Seattle
and the windows rattled
and the roof fell in.

With all the dust and plaster
she looked like a little white-haired old lady,
and the school wouldn't have her,
and she was forced to wander
the earth with her piano
on a flatbed truck
even in foul weather

and sing to two or three little children
on the muddy roads of Africa
and China and Madagascar.

O me, O my, O rode-e-o.
O my, O me, O Robinson Crusoe.
All there's to eat is peanut brittle,
And a sip of the swift, brown Congo.

But then she went to Sudan
and joined a runcible band,
a flute and a harp and a fiddle,
two larks and a snail (for rhythm).
And they played Aswan and Morocco

and Paris, Madrid and Sumatra,
till she landed her helicopter
on the front lawn and stepped out
in a splendor of diamonds
and bracelets and dollars,
and all was forgiven.
She'll enter Third Grade tomorrow.

PS: And the neighbors moved back from Seattle.

Riddle

Emily Rose
was not a Bloom.

Croak

Arnold Craven
was a raven.
But he went to school on the bus
with the other kids,
though he sat on the driver,
and was never late to class
except in the winter
when the teachers shut the windows.
But he spoke with a croak,
for instance, croak croak (nod) croak
(nod) croak croak croak.
And the teachers said this was disruptive,
so he was assigned not to a seat
but to under the coats in the closet with a flute.
So now when a question was passed in to him,
for instance, what is the capital of Great Britain?
he would play a few bars of "London Bridge Is Falling Down,"
and the whole class would clap.
So Arnold wanted to quit school
unless he could go to a raven school.
But there was only one in Nevada,
and his parents couldn't afford it.
So he moped and wouldn't eat his seeds,
and his parents wouldn't take him out for roadkill
because they were afraid he wouldn't fly up quickly enough
if an automobile suddenly rushed down on them.
Arnold began to moult out of season and cried

and had to be taken to school in a cage
and wouldn't play anything but "The Prisoner's Lament"
on his flute, so he was in danger of flunking
everything. He was already flunking Gym
because the other kids said flying wasn't fair,
especially in events like the thirty-yard dash
and the high jump, so he hopped and always came in last.
He couldn't hold a bat because whenever he picked it up
in both claws, he fell over flat.
I wish I would croak, he'd whisper every night
before he climbed into bed. But then the school was afflicted
with head lice, and the only song anyone could sing,

even the teachers, was "Itch, Itch, Itch"
and after that, "Scratch Scratch Scratch,"
until Arnold flew onto the principal's head
and working incredibly fast, ate all the lice.
For four days Arnold flew from class to class—
But oh, the story isn't true, it was only Arnold's dream,
and he was miserable for many years,
a raven misplaced among children;
he didn't even have a date for the Senior Prom.
It was only when he was 24 (which isn't as long
as you imagine, because ravens generally live longer than humans),
moping one day along a cliff in the Catskills,
he met a lady raven named Emily,
and they built a nest and lived happily ever after.
When the first little raven was ready for school,
Arnold swooped down and plucked a diamond ring
from a climber's finger. Neither Arnold
nor any of the other ravens, even the oldest ones,
thought it was stealing,
because before the humans had come,
the ravens had been able to live anywhere in New York State,
and now look at Binghamton and Elmira and Manhattan,
Buffalo and Albany and most of Long Island,
all covered with macadam.
The ravens thought, The humans *owe* us.
So all Arnold and Emily's fledglings
could go to a raven school in Nevada,
not to some school where nothing useful
was taught, not even *Basic Croak*
or *Gathering Berries on a Snowy Winter Morning*.

After the Summer and
the Joys of Ripening

Emily Radish
and Emily Squash
and Emily Potato
were vegetables;
they expected to be eaten.
Still, they had preferences.

Emily Radish didn't want to be eaten by an infant,
because she was tart and might be spit out;
no respectable vegetable likes to be spit out
with a loud YUCK! Salt?
Emily Radish could take it or leave it.
She felt she was sufficient by herself,
but if a customer wanted salt,
she would not try to roll under the table to escape it.

Emily Squash
didn't want to be mashed.
It would take away her pleasing shape
and might mix her seeds with her pulp;
it wasn't natural.
Did she object to little girls drying her seeds
on the windowsill and stringing them on a thread
as a necklace? Well, perhaps that was the best
she could hope for. She certainly didn't want
to be fed to the birds.

And Emily Potato? mashed, fried or boiled?
She wondered if she was going to be left in the bin
until pale sprouts grew out of her eyes
and caught at hands that reached under the counter?
If you'd put me in the ground,
Emily Potato would cry, I could have had children.
I could have fed Ireland. Instead I've been useless.
No, no, murmured the oldest potato of them all;
he had gone soft in the middle
and so could only whisper. We're going to the hogs.

Emily Omelet

Emily Omelet
didn't like eggs.
Why can't I be called SUCCOTASH!
she screamed at her mother.
Or SausageAndRolls.
Or even Vomit.
Or—she looked malicious.
—something worse.
What's worse? said her father,
looking over his newspaper.
But the words caught in Emily's throat.
And she had to be carried to the hospital
in her grandmother's second-best coat.
But while there, she was allowed to change
her name to whatever she pleased,
and so went back to school,
with her nose in the air,
as Emily Cheese.

Three Older Sisters

Emily Best
was not—and yet not the worst
either; she was a middling sort
and yet not to herself;
to herself, to herself—
she didn't know; she was all she had,
whether good or bad;
she began to weep;
she was all alone and full of doubt.
(She could stand on her head if you held her feet.)
To myself I'm precious,
as precious as jewels;
perhaps that's enough
till I grow up;
then I'll become . . .
something else—
But what? She was very fond
of Sara Crewe, who lost all her money
but turned out
to be a princess with a monkey
and buns with jam every night for supper.
But Emily had always lived in the same house
with the same two parents and three sisters,
none of whom were terribly mean.
But she still could be a long lost princess.
That was the point of being long lost:
nobody knew it, not even yourself.

Emily, called her mother,
you forgot to do the dishes.

It was hard to imagine
how a princess would do the dishes.
Perhaps with grand gestures
which spattered her sisters.

Emily slowly twisted
and untwisted on the swing.
If she were a long lost princess,
she'd be an orphan,
without any sisters.
Mother wouldn't be Mother.
Daddy wouldn't be her father.
She began to cry. Emily!
said her mother, carrying
the laundry basket. Why are you crying?
If I were an orphan,
she sobbed, you wouldn't be *my mother*!

Sillinesses

Emily had a nose
and two feet
and could recite the alphabet to b
and multiply six times eight
if the answer was fifty-two,
and knew Madagascar
was in Egypt
when the sun turned green.
This was so astonishing
that the mayor came calling
and had tea with cream
which Emily served on all fours,
using her back as a table
like an elephant in India
when the Maharajah of Cawnpore
gave a party for his nephews,
long before you or I were born
or even thought of.

Harum-Scarum

Emily Jane
ran about in the rain
till her hair was sopped and bedraggled.
Then she went to school as a dragon.

Emily Jane
had never been to Spain,
but she claimed to speak the language:
Gobbledygook gobbledygook!

Emily Jane
hummed a haunting refrain,
>The pigs have eaten the parsley,
>the cows are in the barley.
>There's nothing to eat but knuckle suck
>and the salt of the sea on the heather.

Emily Jane, Emily Jane,
why are you naughty and moody?
In private I'm nice
and eat all my rice,
but in public I'm *asifatooty*.

Berry Berry Sad

Emily
was as sad as a blueberry
and as sour as a cranberry
because blackberry
seeds were stuck in her teeth.
She tried her fingers
and a thorn from a bayberry
and a mashed cherry,
but nothing worked,
until Grandpa got a stick
and whittled a toothpick
and Emily held open her lips
with her fingers,
and Grandpa fiddled,
while Emily talked like this,
Dun tab me!
I mell blid!
Granfa! Granfa!
Dun tade me taw ta denfish!
Grandpa set her on her feet.
All done.
Emily explored with her tongue.
There's still one.

The North Wind
in the Leaves

Emily Rose
wouldn't wear clothes.
A towel and a pin
will do for me.
I'm only three.
Why do I need a dress and shoes?
But when she was six,
playing pick-up-sticks,
the wind snatched her towel
and carried her off
to the Desert of Dis.

So, children, please,
if you must wear a towel
like Emily Rose—
still wand'ring alone
in a robe of dead leaves
and a hat of a scrap
of that unfortunate towel—
sew a rock in both ends
to hold yourself down
when the wind comes along
from the motherless hills
with its fatherless moan.

Reckless Impatience

Emily Phlox
hated clocks.
I won't be told when to do what
by a stupid machine.
I'm a human being.
Does a clock ever know what a moment *means*?
Tick tock, tick tock.
I hate calendars too.
Everybody throws them up in your face.
You're 10; George Clooney is 48;
it's totally unsuitable.
Time is cruel,
whether years, months, days, hours or minutes.
I hate seconds too.
They're like handcuffs.
Emily marched around her room with one fist in the air
like a revolutionist.
I won't be time's slave anymore!
Onward! Upward!
She didn't throw her clock out the window
because she was afraid it would hit somebody,
but she opened it up and took off the hands.
Now it's still running but it doesn't mean anything,
it's stupid. And futile.
Ha. Ha. Time, where are you now?
Not in *my* room!

And outside her room after that she was never *on time*,
but always *early*! or *late*!
Until her mother pointed out that someone who is early or late
is still . . . a *prisoner of time*!
You can't escape, said her mother. What about night and day?
And the seasons. And getting taller.
Or fatter, thought Emily maliciously,
watching her mother trying to button her blue jeans.

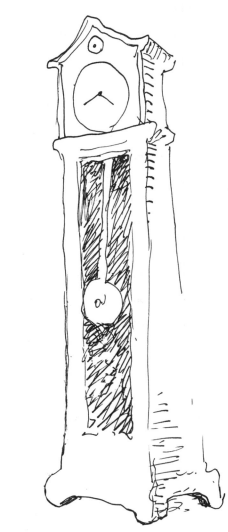

I know for a *fact*, said Emily, that you're 42,
but you've been saying you're 39
since I was in *first grade*!
Snot, said her mother, comes in small packages.
Do you want to eat your dinner in the *pigsty*!?!
We don't *have* a *pigsty*! screamed Emily.
Then, said her mother in a quiet vicious voice,
I'll *make* one. There's still two hours
until dinner. And she went downstairs to the kitchen.
Emily heard cabinet doors slamming, pots and pans,
the back door opening and shutting.
A very strange voice said, Ma'am, we don't carry that brand
of hog. But I've got a couple of right smart Polands.
So Emily went into the kitchen with her head down
and said, I'm sorry. Her mother dialed the phone
and said into it, Cancel the pigs and the swill.
For now.
So I'm just supposed to give in to everything,
said Emily. Perhaps you should start smaller,
said her mother. Not time, perhaps, but dirty feet.
My feet aren't dirty, said Emily.
So see how easy it was, said her mother.
Don't take on the universe till you're older,
like 13. Then Emily knew she was being laughed at.
So she went up to her room and crayoned a big sign:
My mother isn't 39, she's 52!
And tomorrow, if she dared,
she'd wear it to school.

You and Me

Emily Slam
was on the lam
in a skirt with a slit
and a poufy hat.
She wasn't a crook
but she was overdue on six library books
and her name had been in the paper.
Is it costume day? her mother asked.
Have you ever been *arrested*? Emily whispered.
How horrible, said her mother. Never.
But her father was sympathetic
and said she could live in the woodshed
and pretend she was her cousin from Peoria.

But the cousin was 37
and Emily was only 8,
so they gave her a boa
and her great grandmother's pearl-studded cigarette holder
so she could threaten the police
with secondhand smoke if they came to the steps
to get a closer look.
But now she was a truant too,
and who was the Truant Officer?
A great shaggy white dog with a slobbery mouth,
and he always jumped up to smell the truants out.

Emily looked out the cellar window.
The Truant Officer and the Librarian were coming down the street!
And there was a Polar Bear with them!
from the *Federal Department for Cruelty to Little Children*!
Emily hadn't even known they had one!

So they all played cards to see who'd win,
and the last card was dealt, the ace of kings,
the fatal ace! But to whom it was dealt
Emily never found out, for the Mayor rode up
on his ramping horse and called them all
to their senses at once. You must all agree
that less is more if none at all
is considered too! So tea was served.
The gathering dusk obscured the lawn.
Much Later came, and with it was gone
all but us, you and me. And what have we had,
I mean, *really had*, to do with all this?

The New School

Emily Grief
could get no relief:
she didn't look good in lipstick.
At least her mother made her take it off
the first day of third grade.
So she had to get on the bus
feeling naked. She didn't know anyone;
everyone looked at her.
Emily wished she was a potato.

And suddenly she was,
and when she rolled off the bus,
a dog sniffed her,
and the classroom door almost crushed her.
But when people stared at her,
she didn't mind because if *she'd* seen a potato
rolling into Miss Hall's room on the first day of school,
she would have stared too.
When Miss Hall asked everyone what they had done last summer,
Emily said she grew in a field.
The next assignment was to write a poem,
so Emily stood up and recited,

> Boiled potatoes, fried potatoes,
> Jimboree job.
> When I go out to dinner,
> I come back in Bob.

And then it was Riddle Time,

so Emily stood up and said,

> One potato, two potato, three potato, four,
>
> five potato, six potato, seven potatoes more.
>
> What am I?

And no one could guess, but everyone laughed

when she shouted, *Mashed potatoes!*

In History she said that during the Great Potato Famine
everybody's great great great great grandfather
had watched the potatoes rotting
in the fields of Ireland
while eating crickets and grass and even dogs and cats
and so had come to America to eat turkey
and succotash and French fried potatoes with the Indians instead.
And Miss Hall said, Well, it wasn't quite like that
but thank you, Emily.
In Social Studies Emily wrote her paragraph
on *The March of the Downtrodden Potato*,

> Chopped and boiled and fried and mashed,
> pity the poor potato, he has no life,
> baked and roasted and broiled and hashed.
> Rise up, potatoes of the world, rise up,
> do not go gently into the shepherd's pie!

We don't usually allow political poems
in this school, said Miss Hall.
However, that was nice, Emily.
Shall we all say it, class, thrusting up our fists
at the end of each line
as we march around the table?
And so they did, until the loudspeaker said,
Miss Hall. May we have a little more quiet?
Then it was Literature Time, and Emily recited,

> Shall I compare thee to a boiled potato?
> Thou art rounder and don't mash as easily.
> How would you look with a pat of butter
> melting on your head? If I were a fork

and you were a boiled potato, we would get along better
than now when you're just an icky boy.
All the girls laughed, but the boys stamped their feet
until the loudspeaker said, Miss Hall,
must I send Mr. Van Ackroyd?
Mr. Van Ackroyd, the assistant principal,
had once lifted a boy off his feet by the back of his collar.
But then the end-of-school buzzer sounded,
and everyone filed out. As Emily passed
Miss Hall's desk, Miss Hall said, Emily,
we enjoyed having you. I hope you'll turnip
tomorrow. And Emily replied, Rutabaga.

The Swineherd

Emily Briggs
had sixteen pigs
and all of them worked
on an offshore rig,
confined in ingenious cages—
till they grew lean
and swam between
the bars of those erstwhile cages,
appearing one night
by hissing torchlight
as Emily Briggs
was eating ripe figs
and painting her toenails purple.
And now those egregious pigs doze
in heated beds
of savory mud,
while Emily Briggs
maintains the rig
in the wind and snow
and the sharks below
and nothing to eat
but the seeds on the wind
from Trinidad and
Tobago.

Taking Arms Against
a Sea of Words

Abandoned!
Here on a hillside in the forest.
It is like Hansel and Gretel.
Hansel! Hansel! she calls out,
No one comes.
Even a witch would be better than this.
Maybe she is in Poland, where awful things happened.
I'm sure it must just be Halloween, she whispers.
But only a noise like the wind
through an abandoned coal mine answers her.
Then she realizes she has woken up in an abandoned poem.

Even the author had abandoned her.
She had no real beginning or end.
Perhaps if she could just find a rhyme?
But it appears to be an unrhymed poem.
And then she realizes that the only thing real
for miles around is words.
So she stands up and says firmly,

The End